The Agile Meeting Toolkit

100+ simple ways for Scrum Masters to **energise** Agile meetings and **engage** Agile teams

Ethann G. Castell

www.SchoolOfInnovation.net

ISBN-13: 978-0-6488075-0-6

To Louisa,

We are meant to be together.

xx

Table of Contents

Transform Ordinary into Outstanding

Novelty has charms that our minds can hardly withstand.

~William Makepeace Thackeray

Sometimes it seems like Agile has taken over the world. According to the 13th annual CollabNet VersionOne *State of Agile* report, 97% of organisations are now practising agile development.

For many organisations, Agile has become embedded as the preferred way of working. It allows teams to work more collaboratively, respond faster to change and ultimately deliver more business value.

Cadence

One of the critical benefits Agile brings is to introduce cadence to teams. Cadence refers to the rhythm of work, the regular work cycles which occur in Agile, otherwise known as Sprints, and the regular Agile meetings which take place within these Sprints.

Agile meetings

Most Agile teams have a set of regular meetings, and while there are variations to these practices, they include the following four sessions:

- Planning

- Standup (Scrum)
- Review (Showcase)
- Retrospective

Boredom creeps in

For all the benefits that cadence brings, repeating the same process over and over many times can cause boredom and monotony creep in and erode the value the meeting would otherwise provide.

The challenge for the Scrum Master becomes how to continue to reap the benefits from cadence, but also keep the team invigorated and highly involved in their meetings?

Novelty to the rescue

The solution to prevent boredom and increase engagement is to periodically introduce some novelty to the Agile meetings, to add some fresh energy to the meetings.

Why should novelty be important? Because an essential area of our brain is hard-wired for novelty-seeking stimuli. Neuroscientists call it the *substantia nigra/ventral segmental area*, or SN/VTA, and it underperforms if we don't supply it with enough novelty.

We should also consider that about half of the population are extroverts, and there is evidence to suggest that extroverts will tire quickly from repetitive tasks, but become energised by novelty. Introducing novelty may help engage extroverts who otherwise lose interest with too much repetition.

Lastly, my experience of leading and coaching Agile teams has also shown that adding variety (such as the techniques described in this book) can help team bonding, improve team performance and make the working environment a lot more fun.

Who should read this book?

This book is for Scrum Masters and anyone else who facilitates Agile team meetings.

This book is instantly usable. You may like to read it end-to-end, but you can also just dive in and select a technique that looks interesting and try it out.

Consider cultural norms

Keep in mind that some of the ideas presented here may not be suitable because of organizational or cultural norms, the background of the team members, or the stage of team evolution.

Bruce Tuckman's Team Development Model Teams describes how teams go through an evolutionary progression comprising four stages:

- Forming
- Storming
- Norming
- Performing

As groups move through these stages, their dynamics will vary along the way. In particular, the level of trust will increase as the team develops. As the dynamics of the team develop, they may become more open to trying more adventurous meeting techniques.

The age and maturity of the team will also affect which of these techniques may apply.

Respect your people

While globalisation continues to spread, there are still significant differences in cultural norms across the planet. Even within one city, there can be markedly different levels of acceptable behaviour from one organisation to another.

Many workplaces now feature people from a variety of ethnic, cultural, and religious backgrounds, and we must be sensitive to these central aspects of people's lives.

Please consider what is appropriate in your context with the particular individuals involved. You need to decide for yourself whether any technique is suitable for your specific situation.

While I believe that it is an excellent idea to encourage people to stretch a little and move outside their comfort zones, it's also essential to respect individual rights.

Be careful not to force anyone to take part in a way that makes them feel too uncomfortable. There will always be another opportunity for someone to stretch themselves, but only if you still have that person's trust.

Credit where it's due

The ideas and techniques in this book come from a variety of sources, including my experience and thoughts.

I've done my best to acknowledge when the material comes from an existing source, but I may have missed some sources in error.

If you believe that I owe you credit for an idea, then please accept my apology and contact me so I can update the next version of this book.

How this book Is structured

This book contains several chapters, each of which mirrors one of the four core Agile meetings.

It starts with an additional section called *All-purpose Techniques*, which covers ideas and techniques for use in any of the sessions.

Each chapter lists ideas in alphabetical order, so you might need to dig around a little to find something to suit your taste.

Supplementary Book Resources

You can download free Agile meeting templates, guides and more from www.SchoolOfInnovation.net.

Too much of a good thing

In cooking, a little spice can turn a great dish into a masterpiece, but too much can lead to a creation that no-one can stomach. And the same applies to these techniques. My recommendation is to use these techniques sparingly to get the best effect.

There may be a temptation to introduce these techniques to teams on a scheduled basis, such as one new technique every week.

I suggest that you will better results, more bang for your buck, by introducing them irregularly. You will achieve higher novelty value by implementing them at unexpected and irregular intervals.

Experiment

In Agile, as in life, not everything you try will be a winner. Some techniques will work well for your team and others, not so well. So, you must experiment to find out what works best in your situation.

Have fun

I do hope that this book leads you towards higher performing teams and having more fun at work. Because life is too short not to have some fun every day.

Now let's make those meetings outstanding!

About the author

Ethann Castell is an Agile Educator, Coach, Author, Traveler, and the Creator of The School Of Innovation who has his sights on empowering companies to master the art of pragmatic agility and team-centred innovation to ensure lasting success. In addition to his relentless passion for all things agile and 10+ years' worth of industry expertise, he holds an MBA and an array of certifications in the areas of Agile, Design Thinking, Training Design, and Delivery. To find out more about Ethann and his thriving education platform, visit his official website at www.SchoolOfInnovation.net

All-purpose Meeting Techniques

Variety is the spice of life.

~ unknown.

These all-purpose techniques can invigorate most types of Agile meetings.

1. Answer On Behalf Of

In an Agile meeting, the team member answers questions such as "What did you achieve yesterday?" themselves.

One quick way to energise sessions is to have team members answer on behalf of another team member.

You can implement this in a variety of ways, including:

- Team members pair up and describe their answers to their partner, who then presents them to the rest of the team.

- Team members write bullet points on cards and then pass those cards to the team member to their left, or their right, or a random team member. The receiving team member then reads out the points on the card to the rest of the team.

2. Dot Voting

Dot Voting can be great for gauging the team's perspective on relative priorities or preferences. Try Dot Voting the next time your team must make a group decision.

Place all options (on cards or sticky notes) on a wall.

1. Give each team member a set number of voting dot stickers (typically 3 – 5 votes/stickers)

2. The team members place dot stickers next to the options they like. *

3. The option(s) with the most dots are the winners.

* There are two variations on dot voting.

A. Place only one voting dot on an alternative.

B. Place as many voting dots on an option as you like, including placing all dots on only one option.

3. Fist Of Five

Fist Of Five is a technique for gathering a quick reading of the team's feelings on a topic or question.

Each team member rates the item on a scale from 1 to 5 and expresses their rating by holding up their fist with the same number of fingers extended.

For example, a closed-first with only the thumb extended would show a one. An open first with thumb and all fingers spread would mean a five, and so on.

Scrum Masters can gauge a team's confidence-level about an outcome using this technique, for example, assessing the team's confidence in achieving the Sprint goal.

4. Freestyler

Try changing the style of the meeting. Instead of sitting down in the same meeting room, consider these alternatives.

- Breakfast meeting at a local café or restaurant
- Coffee meeting at a local café or coffee shop
- Lunch meeting at a local café
- Dinner meeting at a local restaurant
- Meet while having a drink at a local pub or bar
- Pot-luck meeting – everyone brings a dish to share
- Walking meeting – meet while walking around the neighbourhood or a nearby park or beach.

5. Get The Team Together

For remote or distributed teams, try to get the team together in one physical place at the same time.

Achieving this can take some planning, but the act of getting together in the same physical space, even as a one-off event, can significantly improve team dynamics.

6. Group Selfie

Take a selfie at the beginning or end of the meeting. Perhaps post it on your team wall or internal social media site (Yammer, Teams, Slack, Facebook At Work).

Take the selfie when you are using another technique, such as *Loud Shirt*.

7. Hello Goodbye

Choose a spoken language from a unique culture or country.

Start the meeting by teaching the team members to say hello in that language, and then end the session by having the team members say goodbye in that language.

For example, if you chose the African Bantu language Swahili, then you would open the meeting with *Hujambo*, and close the meeting with *Kwaheri*.

There are thousands of languages spoken across the globe, so you have plenty of variety from which to choose. Here are a few to get you started:

- Japanese: Kon'nichiwa!/Sayonara!

- German: Hallo!/ Auf Wiedershen!

- Spanish: Buenos dias!/Adios!

- French: Bonjour!/Au revoir!

- Italian: Ciao!/Ciao!

- Arabic: Ahlan!/Ma'a as-salaama!

- Dutch: Hallo!/ Tot ziens!

- Mandarin: Nĭ hăo!/Zàijiàn!

- Korean: Annyeong!/Jalga!

- Greek: Geia!/Anito!

- Korean: Annyeong!/Jalga!

- Hindi: Hailo!/Alavida!

- Croatian: Pozdravite!/Pozdravite!

8. Icebreaker Question

Icebreaker Questions can add novelty to meetings, help with team building, and can also be just plain fun.

Start the session with an icebreaker question and have all the team members answer in turn.

Hint: Combine with *Answer On Behalf Of*.

Some example questions include:

- What is your favourite movie?

- What town did you grow up in?

- When you were eight years old, what did you want to be when you grew up?

- Which meal are you best at preparing?

- Which animal are you most similar to?

- If you could be in any movie, what would it be and what character would you play?

Consider making the questions more open, for example, by adding *why* to the subject. Doing so can get people to open up and share more. For example:

Which animal are you like, and why are you like that animal?

See icebreakerideas.com for hundreds of more question ideas.

9. Intrigue

While waiting for the team to arrive at the meeting, display an interesting visual on the screen, something that will create intrigue amongst the team members.

The visual could be an animal, a meme or a short comic. The trick is to find an image that doesn't spark too much off-topic conversation.

You should also change the image routinely or randomly, so people wonder what they'll see next.

Source: the laserfiche.com blog.

10.   Last Word

Last Word is an exercise that takes place near the end of a meeting but importantly before everyone leaves. It can be an effective way of getting people to share their feelings about the meeting which has just taken place.

Ask each attendee to describe their perception about the meeting in one word. Have them record that word on a post-it or card.

Collect the words from the participants and place them on a wall, grouping the cards into themes if applicable.

Read all of the terms out loud to the team.

Ask for a volunteer to share more about their word.

Source: Mayra Souza.

11. Late Penalty

Everyone seems to get busier by the day and turning up for a meeting late is eventually unavoidable for even the most punctual amongst us.

But having people regularly turn up to meetings late can be a real nuisance. So, **as a team,** you may introduce a penalty for latecomers. Remember to keep it fun, and **all** team members must agree on the fine.

Some ideas I've seen or used for a penalty include:

- Gold Coin – in some countries this will be a $1 or $2 coin. Funds could go towards a team social event or a charity of the team's choice. The best thing about the gold coin method is that the team member doesn't have to interrupt the meeting by making an apology. They can simply walk into the meeting and deposit the coin.

- Rubber Chicken – late team members, have to hold a plastic rubber chicken for the duration of the session. Note that this may back-fire in some teams as they may enjoy holding up the chicken!

- Dance – late team members must dance for the rest of the group.

- Doughnuts – serve doughnuts or other food but only until the scheduled meeting start time. The penalty is missing out on the doughnuts. Of course, you could substitute doughnuts with any other food, but it needs to be something that people like and will feel like they have missed out on if they turn up late.

- Latecomer's Hat. Latecomers need to wear a unique late-comers hat for the duration of the meeting.

Source: Kane Mar from Scrumology.

12. Learn Something New Every Day

Introduce a fun, quirky fact at the beginning of each meeting. For example:

Although hippopotamuses might look a little chubby, they can easily outrun a human.

A variation on this is for individual team members to take turns at researching and presenting the fact(s).

Here's a starter list of facts to get you going.

- Nearly 10 per cent of all of a cat's bones are in its tail.

- The national animal of North Korea is the Chollima, a mythical winged horse that they made up.

- Snoop Dogg and David Beckham are such good friends that Snoop sends Beckham his new music before it's officially released.

- A Canadian man named Joel Ifergan lost out on $13.5 million lottery win because his winning numbers were printed 7 seconds too late.

- In patients with nerve damage, their skin doesn't get wrinkly when submerged in water.

- English drummer Phil Collins was the only artist to perform at both Live Aid 1985 benefit concerts. He played at Live Aid Wembley, went by helicopter to Heathrow, flew to New York on the Concorde, then another helicopter to Live Aid Philadelphia.

- The fastest recorded raindrop was 18 mph!

- Abe Lincoln was a professional wrestler long before he became the 16th President of the United States.

- Peanuts aren't nuts! (They're legumes.)

- One million Earths could fit inside the sun!

- William Brewster, the leader of the Plymouth Colony in America, named his children Jonathan, Patience, Fear, Love, and Wrestling.

- When you turn 100 in Japan, the Prime Minister sends you a silver cup to celebrate. So many people are turning 100 that they had to find a way to make cheaper cups.

- All "Granny Smith" Apple trees are clones (grafted not grown) of a single tree in Australia.

Still short on facts? Check out these two great sources:

- Thefactsite.com
- Facts.net

13. Loud Shirt

Have all team members wear a loud shirt for the meeting or the entire day.

By loud, I mean bright, outrageous, definitely not in style, or otherwise in poor taste.

Perhaps make it a competition for the most garish shirt with a special prize for the winner.

Alternatives to loud shirts include big hats and flashy ties.

14. Micro-Timebox

Try to have a micro-meeting – a meeting within a significantly reduced timeframe.

If your Sprint Planning usually is 1 hour, then try to do it within 15 or 20 minutes. You'll probably need someone to be a judicious timekeeper, and you might not be able to let the meeting be as free-flowing as it usually is; someone might need to step in to keep the meeting moving forward.

Consider running a quick retrospective after have a micro-timeboxed meeting. What was it like for the team? Did they learn anything?

Sometime teams will be surprised to discover how much meeting time they usually waste on insignificant or irrelevant topics!

15.   Mood Food

Bring food to the meeting. Doughnuts, fruit, lollies, biscuits. *Try* to make it healthy ☺

Consider taking it in turns and maybe have people bring a home-made treat.

For one team I used to do a cronut run once a month for a team in Sydney, Australia (a cronut is a cross between a croissant and a doughnut - Google them!). I had to go a little out of my way to get cronuts from a particular café, but WOW was it worth it as they were excellent. From that point on, our monthly cronut Fridays created a high level of anticipation and excitement amongst the team.

16.   No Toys Allowed!

In this connected and increasingly fast-paced world, people are spending more and more time multi-tasking. Meeting attendees will often attend to other duties during a meeting such as emails, chat, or working on reports.

With the *No Toys Allowed* technique, for *one* meeting, everyone agrees to turn off their smartphones, put away their laptops and tablets, and just focus 100% on the meeting at hand.

17. Pair Facilitation

Most Agile meetings have one person facilitating the event. You can mix things up a little by having two facilitators work as a pair.

This paired-facilitator could be another team member, which can be an excellent opportunity for someone within the team to build new skills. Or the co-facilitator could be a special-guest facilitator from within or outside your company.

18. Plate of Origin

This technique is one of my all-time favourites.

Many teams include people from a diverse mixture of ethnic and geographical backgrounds. And of course, that means they eat a wide variety of tasty exotic and exciting food preferences.

Plate of Origin is a shared pot-luck meal where each team member brings traditional food from their place of *origin*; the place they were born, or from the area in which their parents were born.

The *place* can be the country people were born in, or for larger countries, the *place* may be the state or region in which they were born.

I want to pass on two pieces of advice from my experiences with this technique.

First, make sure to identify any spicy food (as in HOT spicy). I have been caught out badly on this one, much to the delight of some team members!

Second, check if anyone in the team has any allergies or food intolerances. You may need to make up food labels to identify which foods contain particular ingredients. Common problem areas include:

- Nuts and peanuts in particular.
- Gluten (gluten intolerant)
- Fish, shellfish or seafood (common allergies)
- Diary (lactose intolerant)
- Meat (for vegetarians)
- Animal products (for vegans)

19. Quotes

“

”

Start the meeting with an inspirational or famous quote to set the tone for the meeting. Perhaps you can tie the quote into something relevant to the current team, project or Sprint. Here's one of my favourites which is related to the start of a project.

"Start by doing what's necessary; then do what's possible, and suddenly you are doing the impossible."

~ Francis of Assisi

Here are a few more quotes to get you started:

- You miss 100% of the shots you don't take. –Wayne Gretzky

- I attribute my success to this: I never gave or took any excuse. – Florence Nightingale

- An unexamined life is not worth living. –Socrates

- Eighty per cent of success is showing up. –Woody Allen

- Every child is an artist. The problem is how to remain an artist once he grows up. –Pablo Picasso

- Start where you are. Use what you have. Do what you can. –Arthur Ashe

- "Do what you can, with what you have, where you are." – Theodore Roosevelt

- Fall seven times and stand up eight. –Japanese Proverb

- A person who never made a mistake never tried anything new. – Albert Einstein

- "Be yourself; everyone else is already taken." – Oscar Wilde

- "If the plan doesn't work, change the plan, but never the goal." — Author Unknown

- "You must be the change you wish to see in the world." — Mahatma Gandhi

There are many useful quote websites out there, including:

- quotery.com

- brainyquote.com

- quotegarden.com

20. Reorder The Team

The order of participation in a team meeting can sometimes fall into a specific pattern, which then gets repeated every time.

People often have their usual place at the standup meetings and develop a favourite location in meeting rooms.

Team contributions can also fall into a clockwise or an anti-clockwise pattern.

You can energise your session by changing the order in which people speak.

There are several ways to determine the speaking order, including:

- Spin a bottle (or pen) to determine the first or next speaker.

- Have each team member select a numbered card and have them speak in order.
- Have each speaker nominate the next person to speak.

21. Rotate The Facilitator

If the Scrum Master usually facilitates the meeting, then consider rotating the facilitator amongst team members from time to time.

Some organisations continually rotate the facilitator so that all team members build experience and increase their facilitation skills.

22. Silent Meeting

Hold the team meeting, or part of the meeting, in complete silence, only using gestures and body movements to communicate.

Ok, I'll admit that this is one that I haven't done myself. If you do try it, then please let me know how you get on.

23.   Somewhere Else

If you always have your meetings in the same location, then move the meeting to some other place.

Even moving to another meeting room, or a different floor in your building can add some variety.

24.   Special Guest

An excellent way to introduce variety into a meeting is to have a special guest. The guest is someone from outside of the team and may not be directly related to the current project.

When the guest attends the meeting; they may give a talk or presentation to your group. Depending on who the special guest is, then they may also facilitate the team meeting.

You can get very creative with whom you invite.

Some suggestions include:

- Scrum Master from another team within your organisation.
- An executive from within your organisation.

- A colleague from an external organisation, for example, a Scrum Master or Agile Coach from another organisation.

- Retired business person.

- Visiting speaker from overseas, who is in town to give a presentation or workshop.

- Local sportsperson.

You can announce that there will be a special-guest facilitator at the next meeting ahead of time. But consider keeping the identity of the person a secret to introduce an element of mystery and to spark the team's curiosity.

25. Start Elsewhere

Meetings often have a regular initiator, so consider changing the person who starts the session. Use some of the ideas from *Reorder The Team* to select who starts.

26. Strike a Pose

Instead of using verbal communication, have the team express their personal feelings on an issue or topic by adopting a physical pose.

For example, strike a pose that reflects the last Sprint.

This exercise can be good fun and best done after the team has built up an adequate amount of trust amongst themselves.

Making a physical representation of their response makes a pleasant change from always using verbal and visual techniques. It can also allow people to express things that they may not do so using other mediums.

27. Swear Jar

The original idea behind the swear jar was that every time a team member swears, or utters a profanity, then they have to contribute monetarily to the swear jar.

Funds raised are periodically spent on meeting snacks, a team social event, or donated to a charity of the team's choosing.

The problem arises, of course, that most teams are incredibly polite and well-mannered and therefore, the swear jar will forever remain empty!

In such circumstances, we can extend the scope of swearwords to include specific terms or buzzwords which the team finds annoying or humorous.

For example, on a recent project, we outlawed the word *component* because the team wanted to take a more business-oriented approach and talk in terms of features rather than components.

So *component* effectively became a swear word for the team and anyone who said *component* had to pay the penalty.

Devious readers may have realised that this can create another team game in parallel whereby you try and trick other team members into saying the banned word. But of course, I'm not advocating that you do this ;)

28. Take it Offline

Most people don't like to waste time in meetings.

One of the worst meeting experiences can be when the meeting content has little or no relevance to an attendee. This scenario can force a team member to sit through a bunch of not-relevant-to-them conversations when they could use that precious time more productively elsewhere.

It's essential to make as much of the meeting content as possible relevant to **all** meeting attendees. There will always be exceptions to this rule, and often there is a benefit to having all team members take part in a conversation, even if the relevance isn't immediately obvious. Typically though, we should aim to ensure that the majority of the content applies to all attendees.

If a discussion becomes applicable to only a small subset of the meeting attendees, then that topic can be taken *offline*; the relevant people can discuss the matter in a separate forum.

When a technology system can no longer connect to a network, we say that the system has gone *offline*.

In a meeting, the network is the communication amongst the team members, and by taking a conversation *offline*, we remove it from the team's communication channel and move it to a private channel.

If you find that a conversation you are involved in is not relevant to most of the group, then you can suggest that you take the conversation *offline* and continue with the rest of the meeting.

For conversations that you are not directly involved in, politely interrupt the conversation and suggest that the participants take their discussion *offline*.

Using this technique can make your meetings much leaner and more efficient. It can also reduce the dreaded feeling that people get after they have wasted time in a meeting.

While this technique is effective in all sessions, it is particularly useful in standups meetings. If problems or issues arise during standup, then they can often be taken *offline*, meaning that the topic is parked, and the team continues to the next item.

Immediately after the standup finishes, the necessary team members get together to resolve the issue, but the rest of the group is free to go about their work.

29. Time Switch

Change the time of the meeting. For example, if you always have your stand-up at 9 am then try 9:15 am, or 8:45 am.

You can make a significant change such as moving from morning to afternoon or a minor change like bringing the meeting forward 15 minutes.

You can also experiment with moving the meeting to the beginning or end of the day.

30.   Yes, No, Meh

A similar technique to the Fist of Five, but used when there are only two options such as *Yes* or *No*.

Ask the question to the team and then get a response from the group by asking for either:

- a thumbs-up (yes or agree)
- a thumbs-down (no or disagree)

Count the number of each response type, and the highest score determines the team's decision.

(Some groups also allow a third option; a flat hand response representing the *meh* response - don't mind, either way, no firm opinion)

 Remember to get this book's supplementary resources from www.SchoolOfInnovation.net.

Planning Meeting Techniques

He who fails to plan, plans to fail.

~ unknown.

In the earlier versions of the Scrum guide, the Sprint Planning session included Backlog Refinement, however many organizations now treat Backlog Refinement as a separate activity, which often reduces the time they spend on Sprint Planning.

This section presents techniques suitable for either Planning or Backlog Refinement meetings.

31. Buy a Feature

Buy a Feature aims to uncover what is truly most valuable for Product Owners. It's a fun way of prioritizing features.

The basis of the game is that you first assign a price to each feature or story.

You then give the Product Owner an amount of money (e.g. monopoly money) but only a limited amount of money so they can purchase only some of the features (enough money to acquire somewhere around 1/3 to 1/2 of the total features seems to work best).

The Product Owner then buys the features they want within the limitations of the money available. Often this process will force the Product Owner to make some tough decisions and genuinely purchase the features that are most valuable to them.

32. Change the Sizing Unit

Agile work is commonly estimated using story points. Story points are a relative estimation with no direct correlation to hours or days.

Many teams have standardized on using the Fibonacci sequence for estimating, and there are many Fibonacci card sets and apps available via the internet.

While a team should build skill using a consistent mechanism for estimating, there may be times when you can break the mould and experiment using a different estimating scale.

There are many other scales you can use, which are only limited by your imagination. Some examples include:

- T-shirt Sizes – Extra Small, Small, Medium, Large, Extra Large
- Coffee Sizes – Expresso, Double-shot, Regular, Grande, All-nighter
- Countries – Monaco, Fiji, Greece, Kenya, Russia
- Climbing – Curb, Flight of stairs, Office tower, Burj Khalifa, Mount Everest

- Dog Breeds – Chihuahua, Terrier, Labrador, Great Dane, Saint Bernard

33. Empathy Mapping

Empathy Mapping is a popular tool used in Design Thinking and Human-Centred Design for gaining deep insights into customer personas.

The goals of empathy mapping are to gain insights into the persona and identify the needs of the customer.

If you don't use empathy mapping as a standard part of your development process, then consider spicing up one of your Sprint Planning sessions with an empathy mapping activity.

For a basic empathy map, take a large piece of paper, or a whiteboard, and divide it into four quadrants.

Label the quadrants Say, Do, Think and Feel. (More advanced variations of an Empathy Map can also include sections for Pain Points and Goals)

Hand the team members some sticky notes for recording their thoughts and then pose a series of questions to the team. Some sample questions include

- What would the user hear in these scenarios?
- What would the user see while using our product in their environment?

- What might the user be saying and doing while using our product? How would that change in a public or private setting?

- What might your user be thinking? What does this tell you about his or her beliefs?

- What emotions might the user be feeling?

- What are some of their worries and aspirations?

The team members then place their sticky notes in the appropriate quadrant on the empathy map. Once this part is complete, then the team can discuss their findings, insights discovered, and how they can better deliver value to the customer.

Source: Dave Gray originally developed Empathy Maps.

34. Future Tweets

Most people have at least heard of the microblogging and social networking service Twitter. *Twuffer* is perhaps less well known. Twuffer publishes tweets on Twitter at a scheduled date and time in the future.

To start the Future Tweets exercise, explain Twitter and Twuffer to the team.

Next get the team members to individually write future tweets about the project, along with a scheduled date and time to release them via Twuffer. Explain that this is all hypothetical – we will not make the tweets live!

Then read the tweets out to the group. This exercise is often much fun but can also uncover hidden assumptions and fears about the future of your project.

Source: funretrospectives.com.

35. Ground Rules

Ground rules are a list of behaviours and guidelines under which a team agrees to operate.

They determine how the team will work together and how people can bring up tough topics and have challenging conversations.

For this exercise, get the team to brainstorm a set of ground rules. Then print out the list and place it on your team wall (or virtual team wall).

The critical success factor for Ground Rules is that all team members must agree to a rule before it becomes accepted. If there isn't complete agreement amongst the group, then the proposed rule doesn't become part of the Ground Rules.

Here are some examples of ground rules from other teams:

- Be on time for meetings!
- All team members are equal.
- Make sure everyone gets heard.
- Restrict email reading or web surfing.

- Each Sprint must have a Sprint Goal.

36. My Worst Nightmare

Ask the team members to imagine their *worst nightmare* about the project or product under development, and then record it using words and images.

Next, have the team members share their worst nightmare with the rest of the team.

For example, if you were designing a new sports drink, the *worst nightmare* sports drink might cause illness or taste terrible.

This exercise allows for some psychological venting but can also produce critical insights and highlight pertinent issues.

Source: innovationgames.com.

37. Name the Sprint

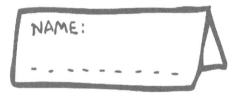

Get the team to come up with a name for the Sprint, something that represents the stage and state of the project.

Perhaps get everyone to suggest a name and then vote with a mechanism such as *Fist Of Five*.

Be sure to add the Sprint name to the team's wall.

38. Planning Poker

Planning Poker is a consensus-based Agile estimating tool. We can use physical Planning Poker card decks or using Planning Poker apps on smartphones.

Each estimator has a pack of planning poker cards with values like 0, 1, 2, 3, 5, 8, 13, 20, 40 and 100. The values represent the number of story points, ideal days, or other units in which the team estimates.

To start a poker planning session, the product owner or customer reads an agile user story or describes a feature to the estimators. The estimators ask questions to gather information needed to estimate.

Once the team is ready, each estimator plays a card to show how complex they think the story is. If there are differences amongst the estimates, the high and low estimators explain why their views differed from the others.

This discussion can uncover valuable information that the other estimators in the team didn't possess.

The team then re-estimates the story, and the process continues until all estimators agree on the same value.

39. Premortem Activity

A premortem is a thought exercise where the team time travels ahead into an imaginary future where the project has been a spectacular **failure**.

The team then works backwards to determine what could potentially lead to the collapse of the project.

The technique enables a discussion about the threats to the project. Having this discussion increases the likelihood of identifying significant risks.

Threats can then be analysed, and preventative actions executed where necessary.

40.   Remember The Future

Remember The Future is a way of identifying likely critical success factors ahead of time.

This exercise is a thought exercise where the team to looks back from an imagined time in the future after the product or project has been successful.

For example, the team might imagine that it is now three months after the project ended.

Ask the group to imagine that they have been using the product for that same period. The product is fantastic, the team is very proud, and the customers love it as it does all they could ever want and more.

Next, get the team to look back to the beginning of the project, and have them describe why the project was so successful both in terms of product features and the project process itself. Discuss the findings amongst the team and identify any critical success factors which emerge.

41. Risky Business

This exercise looks at risks, contingencies and mitigations.

Draw up four quadrants on paper or a whiteboard. Label the X-axis Probability (Low and High), and label the Y-axis Severity (Low and High).

Next, have the team identify risks to the project and place them in one of the four quadrants.

Mitigation is a strategy to avoid the risk occurring. A contingency is a strategy to implement should the risk occur.

Get the team to plan contingency and mitigation strategies for each risk in the top right quadrant – High Probability and High Severity.

42. Split and Recombine

Split the team and the story cards into two or more groups. Have each group work separately on their set of story cards for some time.

Then bring the entire team together and have each team share their analysis with the larger group.

43. Sprint Goal

Sprint Goals focus the team on the deliverables for the Sprint.

If you rarely set a goal for each Sprint, then consider setting a Sprint Goal at your next planning meeting.

The Sprint Goal summarizes the user stories and tasks in the Sprint Backlog. When all the stories within the Sprint are complete, then, and only then, is the Sprint Goal achieved.

Here is an example of a Sprint Goal.

Create a user registration form with fully functional field validation and complete integration into the back-end user database.

44. Tag Team

Get the team to arrange themselves into pairs, and have each pair review a story together.

Then have the couple present the story to the rest of the team.

Encourage the teams to be creative in their presentations. For example, they could present as a wrestling tag team, and tag each other in when it is their partner's turn.

45. Theme

You can energise your Sprint Planning session by adopting a meeting theme.

The theme can draw focus to a particular idea or concept, and you can tie all the team's discussions back to the chosen topic.

Some example themes include:

- Quality
- Value
- Speed
- Visibility
- Completion
- Teamwork

Download your free supplementary resources from www.SchoolOfInnovation.net.

Standup Meeting Techniques

A meeting moves at the speed of the slowest mind in the room. In other words, all but one participant will be bored, all but one mind underused.

~ Dale Dauten.

The Standup (also known as the *Scrum*) is the cornerstone of most Agile processes. Traditionally the standup meeting is held daily and answers three questions:

1. What did you do yesterday?

2. What will you do today?

3. Are there any obstacles impeding you?

While there are many variations on these three questions, the meeting should be short - 15 minutes maximum is the time-box in most organisations.

As the Standup is the most common Agile meeting, it is prone to becoming repetitive and automatic. Therefore, it's a prime candidate for energising!

46. Additional Question

In addition to the three standard questions you ask, try adding a fourth question to the list for one meeting. For example:

- What can we do to complete our highest priority story today?

- Are we working on any hidden tasks that we need to visualise?

- How can we work most effectively as a team today?

- What's the best thing we can do today as a team?

- Have I learned anything I'd like to share with the team?

- How confident are we of achieving our Sprint goal?

- Looking ahead, are there any risks that we can mitigate now?

- What's a wasteful activity that we could eliminate?

- Do I need more clarifications for any feature or story?

- Are we acting on our actions from the previous retrospective?

- Are we ready for the next Product Backlog refinement?

- Are we working on the highest-value stories?

47. Blockers Only

A variation on the daily standup is to focus only on blockers.

When each person in the team talks, they should only talk about things that are impeding their progress and ways to resolve them.

This format can make for a speedy and productive meeting.

48. Different Questions

There are many different variations on the three questions to answer at the standup. Consider using one of the following alternatives.

Alternative 1

- Any impediments in your way?

- What are you working on today?

- What have you finished since yesterday?

Alternative 2

- Things you have done since yesterday's meeting.

- Things you will get done today.

- Obstacles that I need someone to remove.

49. Ending Ritual

Consider adding a specific ending ritual to your standups. This technique will suit some teams a lot more than others.

It could be a simple chant such as

1... 2... 3... Excelsior!

Or something a little more involved, like the following Welsh chant.

Oggy Oggy Oggy!

Oi Oi Oi!

Oggy Oggy Oggy!

Oi Oi Oi!

Oggy!

Oi!

Oggy!

Oi!

Oggy Oggy Oggy!

Oi Oi Oi!

You can Google "Camp songs" for many more song ideas.

You could also add a team gesture like when American football players all place hands together when they end a huddle.

Source: Jason Yip (jchyip.blogspot.com.au/)

50.   Have a Laugh

Start the meeting by reading a joke out loud. Doing so should set a light-hearted tone for the meeting, and the rest of the day ahead.

Perhaps print out a list of puns, or purchase a joke book, and choose one randomly each session.

Please keep in mind the cultural differences mentioned in the introduction and select appropriate jokes.

Because humour varies so much, I won't attempt to provide you with any jokes. But a quick Google search with find thousands that you can use.

51.   Last Arrival Speaks First

Have the person who turns up last to the meeting, speak first. This rule can also act as a great incentive to get people to turn up early to the meeting.

52.   Linked Arms

Instead of just standing in a group, stand in a circle and link arms.

Then conduct the standup as usual.

This method is almost guaranteed to invigorate the meeting.

53.   Monday Morning Special

For a Monday morning standup, when you ask the question, or some variation of, "What did you do yesterday?", literally mean yesterday as in the Sunday.

Get each person to talk about what they did on the weekend just passed. It is a fun way for team members to share more about themselves and their lives outside of work.

54. Morning Song

The Morning Song is a song that you play each morning to indicate that it's standup time.

It can be any song you like but ideally the same song every day so that the team gets accustomed to the music in a Pavlovian way.

One good song to use is *Get Up, Stand Up* by Bob Marley.

Source: Jason Yip.

55. Pineapples

Pineapples is a technique of introducing a *break-word* into meetings.

When the team agrees to use *Pineapples* as a break-word, it can then get the team back on track whenever a conversation has gone off-topic.

During a meeting, **any** team member can call out *Pineapples* to indicate that a conversation has gone on too long, is going around in circles, or needs to be taken offline.

Of course, your team can always come up with a different break-word and that in itself could be a fun exercise.

Source: blog.teamtreehouse.com.

56. Rule of Three

Introduce the "rule of three" to the group.

If a conversation topic goes back and forth three times between two participants, then it is taken offline and discussed outside the meeting.

Anyone within the team can call out a "rule of three", and this can avoid any one person becoming the policeman of the group.

57. Sit Up

As weird as it might sound, try doing the standup while seated. Maybe with the team arranging their chairs in a circle. Ask the group what differences they notice about doing the standup this way?

58. Show Me What You Got

Instead of talking about what they achieved since the last standup, have each team member show their achievements to the rest of the team.

This technique may stretch the meeting out somewhat but is an excellent way of mixing up the daily routine.

59. Sprint Pulse

Take the pulse of the Sprint to determine its health.

Ask each team member to give the Sprint a rating using the *Fist of Five* or an alternative technique. The pulse can be an early warning signal that the Sprint is going off track.

60. Talking Stick

The talking stick is a tradition which comes from indigenous cultures.

Only one person has the stick at a time, and the person with the talking stick is the only one who may talk.

After the person with the stick finishes talking, they then pass the talking stick on to the next person.

The talking stick can be any object you like. Some examples include:

- An actual stick
- Stuffed toy/mascot
- Piece of paper with the three questions written on them
- One-minute timer

61. Thank God It's Friday (TGIF)

For you Friday standup, besides the traditional three questions, ask an additional one; "What do you plan to do tomorrow?" meaning what are they planning to do over the weekend?

Adding this question is another excellent way to build your team by learning more about people's lives.

62. Walk the Wall

Instead of each team member answering the three standard questions, Walk the Wall has the team step through each user story on the Sprint board in turn and discuss the progress and impediments blocking each story.

 Get your free Agile meeting resources at www.SchoolOfInnovation.net.

Review Meeting Techniques

Hide not your talents, they for use were made,

What's a sundial in the shade?

~ Benjamin Franklin

During the Sprint Review, the team demonstrates the progress made during the last Sprint and receives feedback from the Product Owner.

In some organisations, this meeting is called a *Showcase*.

63. Celebrity User

Sprint Reviews showcase working features of the product under development.

The Celebrity User technique asks you to select a well-known celebrity as the imaginary end-user of the product. Then throughout the review, refer to that celebrity as the user of the product.

Let's say for example, that you chose Dwayne "The Rock" Johnson as the celebrity. Throughout the review, you might say things like "When The Rock signs up for an account on our website", or "When The Rock goes to our checkout page."

The Celebrity User technique can not only energise your Reviews but can also offer the occasional unexpected insight.

Some variations on this technique include:

- Only select the celebrity at the beginning of the meeting so that no-one is forewarned.

- Select a famous figure instead of a celebrity

- Select a fictional or cartoon character

64. Customer Attends

Invite one or more customers or end-users to attend the Sprint Review.

Their presence can be the catalyst for valuable interaction between the end customer and the development team.

65. Demonstrators hat

Make it part of the review ritual that whoever demonstrates the product at the review has to wear a particular hat or cap.

If multiple people are presenting at the same review, then the hat needs to pass, and be worn, from team member to team member.

66. Developer Demonstrates

If the Scrum Master or Business Analyst usually demonstrates the product, then get one of the developers to showcase the progress during the review.

67. Movie-themed Presentation

Make the whole Sprint Review meeting a movie-themed event.

Try to tie in the product features, and even the process of building those features, to the selected movie. You can make this as light-on or as over-the-top as you like.

68. Product Owner Demonstrates

Have the Product Owner demonstrate the new functionality back to the team.

69.   Record the session

Record your meeting, or at least the part(s) where you demo the new features, and then post the video it on your intranet or internal social media.

70.   Review retro

The team may benefit from periodically reviewing the review session itself. In other words, to hold a mini-retrospective at the end of the review, about the meeting which just took place.

If the review meetings aren't a positive activity for the team, then this could indicate one of the following common issues:

- The team taking on too much work and not completing it during a Sprint
- The team struggling with existing technical debt
- Features not being developed sustainably to ensure new bugs are not introduced into the codebase
- The team's development practices aren't as tuned as they could be

- The product owner is changing priorities within a Sprint, and the development team is sidelined by scope creep

Partial Source: the Atlassian website.

71. Separate Demo meeting

The focus of the Sprint Review meeting should be about getting feedback from the Product Owner. You inspect the product development done during the least Sprint and determine what adaptions to make during the next Sprint.

In many organisations, the Review has morphed into a demonstration-only meeting with many stakeholders attending, but with minimal to no feedback elicited from the Product Owner.

In such a situation, you might separate-out the demonstration meeting from the review meeting.

One scenario is to have a monthly demonstration for the broader group of stakeholders and turn the end-of-Sprint review meeting into a more intimate session with the Product Owner, focused on gathering feedback.

72. Scene-setting Video

Before starting the review, set the scene by playing a short video.

It could be funny or inspirational but should relate to the features delivered in the Sprint, or the process that has led to delivering those features.

73.   Spanish Inquisition

The Spanish Inquisition was a brutal period in medieval history during which the antagonists tortured thousands of people to extract confessions. And in no way do I want to belittle the suffering which took place during this time.

The Spanish Inquisition is also the subject of a well know comedy sketch by the renowned British comedy group Monty Python. You may have heard the phrase "nobody expects the Spanish inquisition" which originated from this piece.

Sprint Reviews are not inquisitions or courts; they are an informal meeting designed to gain feedback from the Product Owner collaboratively. The team and the Product Owner should work together as partners, and not as adversaries.

Search for "nobody expects the Spanish inquisition" to find one of the many videos of the Monty Python sketch on the internet.

Play the video at the start of the review and share a laugh or two with the Product Owner.

Then you can make a segue from the footage into a reminder this meeting is not an inquisition and that the team and the Product Owner are all *on the same side*. This should set the tone for the rest of the meeting.

74. Tell a story

Make your Sprint Review tell a story, not just of the work completed but also the journey of the team.

Weave a narrative which makes the Sprint come alive and imparts the emotions and sense of accomplishment within the group.

The Sparkol website has a great introduction to classic storytelling techniques.

 Don't miss out on your free Agile meeting resources at www.SchoolOfInnovation.net.

Retrospective Meeting Techniques

The biggest room in the world is the room for improvement.

~ Helmut Schmidt.

Sprint Retrospectives are one of my favourite Agile meetings because I'm a big believer in continuous improvement.

Some teams stop doing retrospectives, but they are the poorer by doing so.

Several of the techniques here are variations on asking for input into one of three categories, for example Good, Bad, Better. While some of these formats seem similar to each other, it is important to note that each variation of the three questions can uncover subtly different information.

75. Agile Principles

Remind each other of Agile principles you each displayed during the last Sprint.

Just in case you forgot, the 12 Agile principles are:

1. Our highest priority is to satisfy the customer

    through early and continuous delivery

    of valuable software.

2. Welcome changing requirements, even late in

    development. Agile processes harness change for

the customer's competitive advantage.

3. Deliver working software frequently, from a couple of weeks to a couple of months, with a

   preference to the shorter timescale.

4. Business people and developers must work

   together daily throughout the project.

5. Build projects around motivated individuals.

   Give them the environment and support they need,

   and trust them to get the job done.

6. The most efficient and effective method of

   conveying information to and within a development

   team is face-to-face conversation.

7. Working software is the primary measure of progress.

8. Agile processes promote sustainable development.

   The sponsors, developers, and users should be able

   to maintain a constant pace indefinitely.

9. Continuous attention to technical excellence

   and good design enhances agility.

10. Simplicity, the art of maximizing the amount

    of work not done, is essential.

11. The best architectures, requirements, and designs

    emerge from self-organizing teams.

12. At regular intervals, the team reflects on how

to become more effective, then tunes and adjusts

its behaviour accordingly.

Ask each team member to write on sticky notes, instances of when their colleagues have displayed one of the principles. Then have team members take turns reading them out loud.

Source: Jesus Mendez (jesusmendez.ca)

76.   Agile Values

Remind each other of Agile values you each displayed during the last Sprint.

Draw four large circles and write one of the Agile core values into each. Here's a reminder of the values:

- Individuals and their interactions
- Delivering working software
- Customer collaboration
- Responding to change

Ask each team member to write on sticky notes instances when their colleagues have displayed one of the values.

Then have team members take turns posting their notes in the appropriate circle while reading them out loud.

77. Appreciation for Others

Most people lead such busy lives these days that we rarely stop and acknowledge those who have helped us.

In this exercise, we press the pause button on life for a few minutes and take some time to recognise our appreciation for the other people in our team.

Get the team write notes of gratitude to the other team members to thank them for something they've down during the last Sprint.

The appreciated act or deed doesn't have to be earth-shattering. It can be something as simple as thanking a team member for keeping the mood in the team light, or for always being on time.

If this is too challenging for your team, then consider making the exercise anonymous perhaps by having people other than the author read out the notes of appreciation.

78. Draw the Sprint

Have each team member draw a visual representation of the Sprint. Inform the team that the drawings can be as realistic or as abstract as they like.

79. ESVP

ESVP is a technique which collects information anonymously about how the team feels about being in the retrospective meeting itself.

Start by dividing a whiteboard or flipchart into four quadrants and label the quadrants:

- Explorer
- Shopper
- Vacationer
- Prisoner

Then explain each category to the team as follows.

Explorer – eager to learn, discover and improve.

Shopper – will review all the available information and happy to leave the meeting with one useful idea.

Vacationer – not interested in the meeting but glad to be away from working at their desk.

Prisoner – feel like they have been forced into the meeting against their wishes.

Next, ask each team member to decide which quadrant they are in and write this on a piece of paper. Have them fold up their piece of paper so that their responses remain hidden.

The facilitator should then collect the responses, tally the count for each quadrant and write the totals on the board near each quadrants title. Make sure you put the papers in your pocket and throw them away later.

Discuss the results amongst the team.

Source: Enrico Teotti.

80.   Famous Team Member

This exercise is especially suitable for teams or team members who have active imaginations.

Have each team member come up with a famous person; it can be anyone living or dead.

Next, have the team describe how that renowned person would improve the current team, or what course of action that person would recommend for the current project.

While this exercise is often much fun, it can also be insightful for some people as it gets them to step outside of themselves and view the current situation from a unique perspective.

If you are having trouble coming up with famous people, then perhaps start with the following list:

- Bill Gates

- Usain Bolt

- Leonardo da Vinci

- Rosa Parks

- Sun Tzu

- Elvis Presley

- Winston Churchill

- Kim Kardashian

- Mahatma Gandhi

- Nikola Tesla

- Jackie Chan

- Nelson Mandela

If you need extra famous, people then check out the list of the 200 most famous people on listchallenges.com.

81. Five Dysfunctions of a Team

The Five Dysfunctions of a Team comes from a 2002 book of the same name by Patrick Lencioni. In his book, Lencioni identified what he believed are the five root causes of dysfunction within a team.

Those dysfunctions are:

1. Absence of trust—unwilling to be vulnerable within the group

2. Fear of conflict—seeking artificial harmony over a constructive passionate debate

3. Lack of commitment—feigning agreement for group decisions creates ambiguity throughout the organization

4. Avoidance of accountability—ducking the responsibility to call peers on counterproductive behaviour which sets low standards

5. Inattention to results—focusing on personal success, status and ego before team success

As a team, discuss the five dysfunctions and identify ways in which these dysfunctions are, or could, affect your current team.

82. Five Whys

The Five Whys is a popular tool for determining the root cause of a problem. It came out of the Toyota Production System (TPS). You can use the Five Whys as part of your Sprint Retrospective to unpack the underlying cause of a problem. Choose a problem (a simple to medium difficulty problem works best) and then ask the question "Why?" five times.

Here's an example.

1. "Why did the robot stop?"

The circuit has overloaded, causing a fuse to blow.

2. "Why was the circuit overloaded?"

There was insufficient lubrication on the bearings, so they locked up.

3. "Why was there insufficient lubrication on the bearings?"

The oil pump on the robot is not circulating sufficient oil.

4. "Why is the pump not circulating sufficient oil?"

The pump intake is clogged with metal shavings.

5. "Why is the intake clogged with metal shavings?"

Because there is no filter on the pump.

Source: Toyota (Toyota.com)

83. FLAP

Drap four columns or quadrants on the board and have the team record their feedback on the last Sprint into the four FLAP categories.

- Future considerations
- Lessons learned
- Accomplishments
- Problem areas

Discuss as a team.

84. Formats

There are many original formats for structuring a retrospective. Changing the meeting format can change things up for the team. Here are a few useful formats with which to experiment.

Classic format

1. set the stage
2. gather data
3. generate insights
4. plan an experiment
5. close the meeting

Seven step format

1. Set the meeting context
2. Review the Prime Directive
3. Team energiser exercise
4. Check-in with each team member
5. Main retrospective activity
6. Filter and collate the information
7. Check-out activities

Source: Paulo Caroli

Ethann's format

This format is my format. I like to break the retrospective into two parts:

1. A fun team-building exercise.

2. Retro

   a) Review the actions from the last retro.

b) Review the Sprint using one technique in this book.

c) Develop specific actions for improvement in the next Sprint and ensure that each action has a team member responsible for it.

85.   Genie in a Bottle

Present the following scenario to the team:

You have freed a genie from being trapped in a bottle fro a thousand years. The genie expresses his gratitude to you by granting you three wishes.

What do you wish for?

Please make

1.   One wish for yourself

2.   One wish for your team

3.   One wish for all the people in the world

No Cheating! (i.e. wishing for more wishes or more genies)

Let everybody present their wishes to the team.

Optionally you can then dot vote on the best or most appreciated wishes.

Source: Özer Özker & Anke Bartels

86. Good/Bad/Better

Use Good, Bad and Better as the focal points of the review.

- Good – what was good about the last Sprint.

- Bad – what was bad about the last Sprint.

- Better – what could be better next Sprint.

87. Helped Hindered Hypothesis

Gather team insights under the headings of Helped, Hindered and Hypothesis.

- Helped – what helped us last Sprint?

- Hindered – what slowed us down or got in our way during the last Sprint?

- Hypothesis – what might make things better next Sprint? What can we try (and test) to see if it improves our process?

88. Keep/Drop/Add

A three-category retrospective format using the categories Keep, Drop and Add.

- Keep – things that worked, and we want to keep doing next Sprint.

- Drop – things that didn't work, and we want to drop from the next Sprint.

- Add – things we should add to the next Sprint to improve it.

89. Last Sprint as a

Pick a category and have each team member describe the previous Sprint as a member of that category.

For example, if the category selected was Animals, then each team member would choose an animal that they thought best represented the Sprint.

Then the team would take turns sharing the animal they chose with the rest of the group and discuss *why* they selected that animal.

Here are some categories to get you started.

- Car

- Animal

- Mobile phone
- Movie
- Book
- Music video
- Superhero
- Video game
- Kitchen Appliance
- Holiday destination
- TV show
- Song

90. Loved, Learned, Lacked, Longed for

Draw up four (category) columns on a whiteboard and label them:

- Liked
- Learned
- Lacked
- Longed for

Have the team identify items from the last Sprint which fit under each category and place them on the whiteboard using post-it notes.

Then discuss as a team.

Source: EBG Consulting (www.ebgconsulting.com).

91. Mad/Sad/Glad

Gather feedback and insights using the categories Mad, Sad and Glad.

With this format, it sometimes helps to label the columns with emoji faces, similar to the images above.

- Mad – what made me angry during the last Sprint.

- Sad –upset me during the last Sprint.

- Glad – what I'm happy we did during the last Sprint.

92. Movie Critic

Introduce the activity by asking the team to imagine that the last Sprint was a movie, and they had to write a review:

- What was the genre of the film (e.g. horror, drama)?

- What was the (central) theme? Describe in 2-3 words.

- Was there a big twist (e.g. a bad guy)?

- What was the ending like (e.g. happy-end, cliffhanger) and did you expect it?

- What was your highlight?

- Would you recommend it to a colleague?

Give each team member a piece of paper and five minutes to silently ponder the questions.

In the meantime, or before the session, divide a flip chart into seven columns headed with 'Genre', 'Theme', 'Twist', 'Ending', 'Expected?', 'Highlight', 'Recommend?'.

When everyone has finished writing, fill out the flip chart while each participant reads out their notes.

Afterwards, look at the finished table and lead a discussion about

- What's standing out?

- What patterns do you see? What do they mean for you as a team?

- Suggestions on how to improve.

Source: Isabel Corniche (@tuedelu on Twitter).

93. Nicknames

Have the team create a nickname for each team member. Remember to instruct the teams to play nicely with this one! Also, make sure that each team member is Ok with the new nickname.

Also, consider printing out name tags with the nicknames on and placing them on each person's workspace.

94. One Word

Have each team member sum up the last Sprint in just one word. Record these words on a flip chart or whiteboard and have each team member explain why they chose that word.

95. Perfection Game

Prepare a flip chart with two columns, a slim column for 'Rating' and a wide column for 'Actions'.

Get the team members to rate the last Sprint on a scale from 1 to 10.

Then they each must suggest what action(s) would make the next Sprint a perfect 10.

Source: Ben Linders (www.benlinders.com).

96. Prime Directive

The more open and honest a team can be, the better the outcome from the Retrospective.

To help get people to be honest and open, we need to create a safe space for people to express themselves.

One way to create a safe space is to use the Prime Directive:

Regardless of what we discover, we understand and truly believe that everyone did the best job they could, given what they knew at the time, their skills and abilities, the resources available, and the situation at hand.

The Prime Directive aims to create a blame-free culture which recognizes that everyone is doing the best they can.

There are two suggested uses of the Prime Directive.

1. Have someone read out the Prime Directive at the beginning of the Retrospective.

2. Print the Prime Directive and place it prominently during the Retrospective as a continual reminder.

Source: Norm Kerth (www.retrospectives.com)

97. RAID

RAID is a technique used for decades in traditional Project Management to identify Risks, Assumptions, Issues and Dependencies.

Create four columns on the whiteboard and label each column with one of the RAID terms.

Have the team identify items falling within each category and place them on the board.

Then discuss as a team.

98.   Random Object Association (ROA)

Random Object Association (ROA) is a technique that can generate some very novel ideas and can also be an excellent source of fun.

You select a random object and then have a team member think about, and then describe how that object could have improved the last Sprint.

I have seen some people struggle with this exercise, so make sure to keep the mood light and allow any team members to pass, or select another object, if they have any difficulty.

If you want to get started immediately then here's a starter list:

- Soap
- Fork
- Perfume
- Paper
- Cup
- Sunglasses
- Stop sign
- Bread
- Pillow
- Hanger

- Water Bottle

- Truck

- Banana

- Flag

- Toilet

- Cardboard box

For more randomness, visit the object generator at www.randomlists.com/things.

99. Rate the Product or Service

This technique is a subtle variation on rating the Sprint that can produce some interesting insights.

Instead of judging the Sprint process itself, rate the product or service that was delivered at the end of the Sprint on a scale from 1 (awful) to 10 (fantastic).

Then discuss as a team.

100. Showcase Email

As a team, compose an email to send to the rest of your organization telling them about:

- Your team
- How well you work together
- What you have achieved
- How you add value to the business.

The exercise is about writing the letter as a team. You don't have to actually send the email to anyone. But you can send the email if the teams decided to.

An even more daring alternative is to send the email to the CEO of your organization!

101. SoMoLo

With SoMoLo the team reviews the last Sprint through the lenses of:

- Same of – we did the right amount if this
- More of – we need to do more of this
- Less of – we need to do less of this.

102. Sprint Rating

Get the team to give the previous Sprint a rating from 1 to 5, where five means excellent and one means mediocre. (Feel free to come up with your own scale).

Then discuss the ratings assigned as a team.

Pay particular attention to any wide discrepancies in scores across the team, and try to discover why there is such a difference.

It can also be interesting to include this as a regular part of your Retrospectives and chart the ratings over time.

103. Start/Stop/Continue

Use the format of Start/Stop/Continue to review the last Sprint.

- **Start** are things that we want to start doing in the next Sprint.

- **Stop** are things that we are doing but want to stop doing in the next Sprint.

- **Continue** are things that are working well and that we should continue in the next Sprint.

104. Super Heroes

Have the team nominate one Super Hero collectively or one different superhero for each team member.

Next, have each person describe how that Super Hero, using their superpowers, could have improved the last Sprint.

Here's an example to get you started:

Super Hero: Wonder Woman

Super Power: Magic Lasoo (which forces people to tell the truth)

Improvement: Wonder Woman could have used her magic lasso on our Product Owner to force them to identify the highest value item, rather than the one they thought would be fastest to develop.

This process can be an effective way of letting off some steam. But you can also then brainstorm ideas about how to achieve the same outcomes the superheroes achieved but as mere mortals.

105. Take a Stand

Take a Stand is a technique to get a sense of everyone's position on an issue and to move towards achieving a team consensus. It's useful when the team can't decide between two options.

Create a big scale (a long line) on the floor with markers or masking tape.

Mark one end as option A and the other as option B.

Next, ask the team members to physically position themselves on the scale, according to their preference for either option.

Have the team members discuss they moved their position on the line. As the discussion takes place, allow team members to move to a different location on the line.

Continue until one option has a clear majority.

Source: Nick Oostvogels.

106. Team Member Awards

Similar to the Story Oscars, the Team Member Awards allow you to create awards for team member performance during the last Sprint.

Here are a few categories to get you started:

- Flash award for the fastest team member, for example, the quickest tester.

- Most Punctual award for the person who is always on time for meetings.

- Silent Achiever award for the team member who quietly gets their work done without being noticed.

- Mission Impossible award for achieving a seemingly impossible task.

- Early Bird award for the person who always starts the day the earliest.

- Happy Puppy award for the one who is always in friendly spirits.

- Extra Mile award for the person who went above and beyond for the team.

- Old Faithful award for the team member who can always be relied upon.

- *Took one for the team* award for the person who stepped up and completed an unpleasant task, for the benefit of the team.

- Night Owl award for the team member most likely to still be in the office late at night.

- MacGyver award - for the person able to solve a problem with almost zero resources.

- Wired award for the person who drank the most coffee or energy drinks.

Have fun with creating new categories but be mindful not to offend anyone.

107. The One Thing

Get each team member to write on a piece of card the one thing they would change about the last Sprint.

Place the cards on a wall and discuss as a team.

108. User Story Oscars

The Oscars is an annual American awards meeting to recognize excellence in cinematic achievements.

User Story Oscars are an awards for User Stories from your last Sprint.

The team nominates stories for awards and reflects on the winners.

Display all stories completed in the previous Sprint on a wall or board.

On a separate board, create three award categories (i.e. boxes on the board):

1. Best story

2. Most annoying story

3. (3rd category created by the team)

Ask the group to 'nominate' stories by putting them in one of the award boxes.

Dot-vote the nominees for each category and announce the winners. Ask the team why they think the user story won in this category and let the team reflect on the process of completing the tasks - what went well or wrong.

You can have fun coming up with your categories but here are a few to get you started:

- Best Horror Story
- Best Comedy Story
- Best Written Story
- Most Challenging Story

Source: Marin Todorov

109. Wedding Retro

A traditional English wedding rhyme from two hundred years ago describes what a bride should wear on her wedding day. The verse goes:

Something old, something new, something borrowed, something blue, and a sixpence in your shoe.

The Wedding Retro format borrows from this rhyme and gathers feedback from the team based on the following categories:

- Something Old - established practices
- Something New - experiments in progress or suggestion of something new to try as a team.

- Something Borrowed – an idea or tool that this team can borrow from another team or website.
- Something Blue – blockers and other causes of distress.

110. Weather Forecast

Either individually, or as a team, create a weather forecast for the next Sprint.

You might want to include the following items in your report:

- Temperature range
- Wind
- Sunshine
- Clouds
- Rain
- Snow
- UV rating
- Humidity
- Fire rating
- Air quality
- Tides
- Phase of the moon

The goal is to identify potential blockers or other areas of concern in the upcoming Sprint.

111. Weather Report

Similar to the Weather Forecast, but this time get the team produces a report about the current Sprint.

112. What, Who, Due

Prepare a flip chart with three columns titled 'What', 'Who', and 'Due'.

Ask one participant after the other, what they want to do to advance the team.

Record the task in the W*hat* column. Then agree on a 'done by' date and let them sign their name against the task.

If someone suggests an action for the entire team, the proposer needs to get an agreement (and signatures) from the others.

113. Worked worked work

Gather feedback on the last Sprint based on the following categories:

- **Worked Well** – help the team make progress

- **kind of Worked** – produced mediocre results.

- **didn't Work** – did not add value to the last Sprint.

114. Wow, Wondering or Worried

Review the last Sprint based on:

- Wow – what impressed us

- Wondering – what puzzled us or was difficult to understand

- Worried – what concerned us or stills concerns us

 Grab your free Agile meeting resources at

www.SchoolOfInnovation.net.

www.ingramcontent.com/pod-product-compliance
Lightning Source LLC
Chambersburg PA
CBHW071300050326
40690CB00011B/2482